Omaha Beach

Oliver Warman

Oliver Warman regularly tours the Normandy Battlefields and this is his second book on the battlefields of 1944.

Le Mémorial de Caen

Esplanade Eisenhower
BP 6261 - 14066 CAEN Cedex 4

Contents

Papers please!

INTRODUCTION

In the grey dawn of a wet Normandy morning, thousands of young Americans climbed down the uncertain, swinging ropes, snaking down from the large transports into the tiny landing-craft that were to take them to the shore five miles away. The sea was rolling with the remains of an Atlantic swell after two days of storm. That shore had been designated OMAHA by the Chiefs of Staff Committee and was to remain forever a name associated with heroism, triumph and disaster in American history. This book attempts to tell the story of that beach on June 6th 1944 based not only on American records but also from more up-to-date German papers. Omaha was, after all is said and written, a German battlefield too. A 19th Century German historian, Leopold von Ranke, exhorted historians to search for facts and desist from opinions. It is this viewpoint that appeals to the author, bearing in mind the paucity of factual reporting.

Frontier crossing - NB the horse transport in 1940

PRELUDE
France in 1940

Hitler's army had come to France in 1940 in a lightning campaign that lasted six weeks during which they penetrated the French defences at the foot of the Ardennes and, leaving some of the infantry divisions behind, drove north towards the French coast. The British Expeditionary Force under Lord Gort was pushed across the Channel with the loss of almost all its equipment: Dunkirk was but the first in a series of setbacks. The capitulation of the French army left Hitler and his Generals in a state of euphoria tempered with an indeterminate static nervousness unable to decide what to do next. Guderian, forever the thinker and doer, had suggested and very nearly obtained approval for a thrust down through Spain to Gibraltar and into the French colonies within North Africa. The euphoria concealed immediately emerging cracks to which few dared to draw attention. These cracks were in the German economy and illustrated the country's inability to exist without imports,food and what can be classified generally as strategic war material. There was only a small rolling-stock industry for the railways and, surprisingly for a country that could later produce the best main-battle tank in the world, a motor-transport industry that was totally inadequate for the country's needs. However this is not to say that the army, for example, was not equipped to a high standard - it was. But the rate of attrition in battle and the expansion of the forces as a whole outpaced the abilities of every part of the war production industry. Perhaps, more curiously, Hitler seemed to have no long-term strategic plan for the prosecution of the war.

The initial German success

Amidst the plaudits of the campaign in Normandy leading up to the eighteen months before June 1944 the Russians had destroyed, in the east, the best part of the German Army: Some two million German soldiers had met their death in a remarkable struggle for domination of the Russian steppes. Set against the magnitude of the Russian campaign the events of Dieppe in 1942 appear insignificant. However that incursion into mainland France, ill thought out as it was, gave the British Commonwealth a foretaste of German prowess on a defended coastline and experience of the handling of an amphibious assault from a base just 70 miles away. The German defenders of Dieppe were the same second-line troops that were to defend Normandy in June 1944.

It was these poor quality troops, who stood their ground, that were to deny the Allies many of their D-Day objectives and gain time for the Panzer Divisions and their supporting Infantry to march up to the battlefield. Thus, at this time-distance of almost sixty years it is almost obvious that there were two ways to defeat Germany: invade the coastline of Europe and expel the enemy forces from their conquests and shatter by bombing their capacity to make war.

Pearl Harbour. SS West Virginia, USS Tennessee and USS Arizona burning

However, to think of this in the bitter years of the early 1940s was clearly visionary, provided of course that the vision included the military and industrial might of the United States of America. When the Japanese attack on Pearl Harbour on 7th December 1941 effectively took the USA into the war as a much needed ally of Britain, the vision became the germ of a reality.

The turn of the tide

Mid October 1942 marked the peak of German success. From thereafter, in early November the British began to not only hold their line but also to push back and defeat Rommel at Alamein. Operation Torch was the final seal of German defeat in North Africa and from there onwards Germany and its Italian vassal were vulnerable on their southern flank. On a far larger scale, in the east, the German 6th Army was utterly destroyed, overwhelmed at Stalingrad in January 1943. German and Roumanian losses were in excess of 150,000 and those of Russia totalled over 500,000. Of the half-million civilian inhabitants of the city a mere 1,500 were left. In late 1942 the sinking of the *Laconia* carrying 1,800 Italian prisoners of war and approximately 1,000 women and children marked a grisly beginning of the end of submarine warfare that was to slacken as the end of 1943 approached. 2,700 Allied Merchant ships had been sunk. 784 German U boats and their crews of 28,000 officers and men were lost. The tide had indeed started to turn.

Infantry by the Red October Factory, Stalingrad

The Allies agreement over a Second Front

This reality, the planning of what was to be known as the Second Front, raised the obvious questions of 'where' and 'when' the answers to which were to take more than eighteen months to materialise. The proposed invasion was at last agreed between Roosevelt, Churchill and Stalin in Teheran in November 1943 and a date set around the beginning of May 1944 by which time the early problems with a lack of landing craft and material would be resolved. Deception started early. As a result of better electronic measures existing in 1943 von Rundstedt and OKW, back in Rastenburg, over-estimated the strength of allied forces in the United Kingdom. Both believed that the heavy concentration of what were ghost formations in north Scotland indicated an invasion of Norway and that Force Patton was forming up in the eastern home counties for an invasion of the Pas de Calais area.

The Atlantic Wall - construction workers

The Atlantic Wall

However, let us return to Northern France. The beach, later to be known as Omaha, formed only a part of Hitler's defence of Fortress Europe. The latter constituted a necklace of fortifications laid around the northern and western coast of Europe from the Spanish frontier to Norway. Hitler hoped that this carefully laid necklace would defeat the anticipated Allied invasion and, whilst administering a psychological shock from which British and American public opinion would never recover, would free him to renew his offensive in the east, in Russia. The general strategic solution against this anticipated Allied attack was to put everything into the shop window and in one large counter-blow force the allies back into the sea. This wall, this necklace of mutually-supporting fortifications began to be built from 1942 onwards by an army of conscripted labour. France provided a large portion of this conscripted labour under a deal, negotiated by Laval (who held the joint portfolios of Prime Minister, Foreign Minister and Minister of the Interior), whereby France would supply labour and Germany would release a proportion of the two and a half million prisoners of war (the releve). In terms of material this conscripted, partially French labour force used some 17.300,000 cubic yards of concrete and 1.2 million metric tons of steel reinforcement the rusting remnants of which protrude from every bunker and fortification that remain. The priority for construction was initially concentrated between the area of the River Seine and the estuary of the Maas but the project for this wall was too large for the resources of the German construction industry and their agent, the Todt Organisation. Furthermore the proposed defences were too extensive for the German army to garrison effectively. The defensive installations were designed, in detail, by Hitler himself. The design included an advanced tactical HQ, for his use, between Soissons and Laon, called W2. (He saw himself commanding the German retaliation should the Allies invade France).The work was constantly interrupted. History, thus, seemed to be repeating itself: *"the most important factor underlying the defeat of Germany in the 1914 -18 war was the inability of the Kaiser and his military and political leaders to understand the limits of Germany's war potential and, in parallel, to appreciate the political and material strength of the enemy coalition".*

Von Rundstedt

The Western part of this Atlantic Wall was under the command of Field Marshall Gerd von Rundstedt whose divisions, many of them 30% under strength, were spread unevenly over the coast and hinterland of France and Holland. Most of these purely defence-divisions, known as Coastal Divisions, were made up of soldiers who had been unable to pass a fitness test. Some were walking wounded on recovery, foreign nationals from Russia and the Balkans but the whole was under the command of a backbone of good Officers and NCOs most of whom had served on the Russian front. By 1943 25% of the German army was over the mid-thirties age group.

The Atlantic Wall, an example of a completed fortification

(left to right)
Sinnhuber,
Speidel,
Rommel

Von Rundstedt's HQ was based at Fontainebleau and he lived, in luxury, in the Hotel George V in Paris. The naval forces under the Admiral Commanding Group West, Krancke, were entirely independent and took their orders from Donitz in Berlin. Krancke, whose forces were almost miniscule compared to those of the Allies, was based in Paris. Also in Paris was Sperrle's Air Fleet HQ which was an organisation that controlled 300 fighters, just under 400 bombers 95,000 anti-aircraft troops and some 30,000 parachutists. Sperrle was responsible to Goering in Berlin. Either,at a whim, could and did remove forces from von Rundstedt's command. There was little inter-service co-operation. In January 1944 Hitler appointed Field Marshal Erwin Rommel as commander of Army Group B, the forces facing the possible Allied invasion threat in Normandy. However he was not master of his own destiny. Subservient to von Rundstedt, he was in control of the area a few hundred yards seaward of the

high water level to some six miles behind the shoreline. It is remarkable that two Field Marshals agreed to this overall untidiness of command. From the very beginning Rommel took the stance that *"We must repulse the enemy at his first landing site...if we don't manage to throw them back at once the invasion will succeed... in North Africa the bombs were dropped in such concentrations that even our best troops were demoralised. If you can't check the bombing, all other methods will be ineffective, even the barriers"* This waterline-strategy, the defeat of the enemy when he was most vulnerable, meant that the Atlantic Wall had to be strengthened further and this he proceeded to do with great energy.The number of beach obstacles were increased, more concrete bunkers were constructed and three new minefields were laid out to sea. However material shortages reduced his demand for fifty million mines to between four and five million and even these were lacking in places.

The waterline strategy adopted by Rommel was bitterly opposed by the Commander-in.Chief West, von Rundstedt. In this opposition von Rundstedt was joined by the Commander of Panzer Group West, General Geyr von Schweppenburg. Neither possessed Rommel's experience of a desert war in which, ultimately, air superiority had prevented the movement of reserves or at least had written down their effectiveness. There were effectively eleven Panzer and Panzer Grenadier Divisions available. Four were south of the Loire, one was located in Holland and six were in Army Group B. Of these six, three - 1SS Pz n Belgium, 12SS Pz in Lisieux and Pz Lehr in Chartres were to be in OKW reserve and formed part of Panzer Group West as did 17 Pz Grenadier. The remaining divisions, 2Pz near Calais, 116 Pz near Rouen and 21 Pz near Falaise and Caen, were under Rommel's operational control but could only be repositioned with the approval of OKW ! This then was the situation on the eve of the invasion on June 6th. Lacking the meteorological back-up of distant Atlantic weather-stations, which would have suggested otherwise, the three commanders on the spot, von Rundstedt, Krancke and Sperrle, all believed that in view of the weather conditions, no invasion was imminent.

Dieppe - the aftermath

THE START OF OVERLORD

The lessons from Dieppe

But let us go back. The ill-conceived Dieppe raid of Saturday, 19th August 42 had engendered even more grave doubts on ROUNDUP which was a plan to invade either a favourable location in the Calais area or the coast of Normandy, because it was plain that the Dieppe Raid had had no effect on the Germans whatsoever. The Germans had managed to repel some of the finest soldiers Canada had produced - 65 % of the eleven assaulting Canadian battalions became casualties. The 2nd Canadian Division ceased to exist. This had been achieved by a minimum of ordinary German soldiers fighting behind indestructible obstacles, well-supported by artillery of all calibres, seemingly impervious to attack by a dominant Royal Air Force on the day. The bravery and the sacrifice of the Canadians was to count for nothing against the well laid out and thorough German defence system. After the event, it was plain that any future landing would have to take place away from a port and its easily fortified buildings, on an open beach, supported by a bombardment so powerful that it would shock any enemy opposition, whether armour or artillery, into total inaction.

*Dieppe
the burning remains*

(left to right) Tedder, Eisenhower, Montgomery

COSSAC and SHAEF

Thus, ROUNDUP was put into storage but the seed conceived OVERLORD, a name selected by Churchill and others from a list kept by the Chiefs of Staff. In March 1943 Lt. Gen Frederick Morgan was appointed Chief of Staff to the Supreme Allied Commander designate. The organisation,

welded together by him, using planners previously involved in BOLERO and ROUNDUP, became known as COSSAC from the first letters of General Morgan's new title. By 27th July, in what was undoubtedly one of the best examples of Anglo-American co-operation, he and his staff had produced an outline plan of the forthcoming invasion. Whilst Morgan was occupied with the many complications and diversions of COSSAC, which would soon cease to exist as such, Alan Brooke was setting up the skeleton of the British commitment to OVERLORD whilst

Bradley and Montgomery Marshall was planning the American side of the operation. The whole would ultimately be under one supreme commander of land, sea and air forces, Eisenhower, with SHAEF the aforementioned headquarters.

The cramped conditions on loading

NEPTUNE

"The object of Operation Overlord is to mount and carry out an operation with forces and equipment established in the United Kingdom... with a target date of 1ˢᵗ May 44, to secure a lodgement on the Continent from which further operations can be developed..." In June 1943 Normandy was selected as the area for the main landings. Since there were no natural harbours capable of supporting the invading force it was decided, at the same conference, that floating harbours would be towed across the channel for use off an American and a British beach. In the time leading up to the invasion, all bridges and rail communications along the Seine and the Loire would be destroyed, leaving the Normandy rectangle comparatively isolated from the rest of France. The die was cast but the foreboding with which the planning staff, and in particular the probable senior commanders, viewed the emerging NEPTUNE-OVERLORD plan during 1943 is underestimated. Perhaps this foreboding is summed up in Alanbrooke's statement in "Notes on my life"...*it may well be the most ghastly disaster of the whole war."*

NEPTUNE, the sea routes

US Coastguard 83 ft fast patrol boat on escort duty

The overall plan for the initial phase of NEPTUNE - OVERLORD was to land Dempsey's 2nd Br Army to the east, on both sides of the Orne, and Bradley's 1st US Army to the west astride the Vire and the base of the Cherbourg Peninsula. These two Armies formed 21 Army Group under Montgomery. The whole, all forces sea, land and air, were under Eisenhower. The spearhead of the assault, the break-in, was a force of three airborne divisions and six infantry divisions which were to be built up to twenty four divisions as rapidly as possible. When this had taken place Patton's 3rd US Army was to pass through Bradley's forces on its breakout south down the western side of Northern France and, turning east, aim for and achieve an occupation of Paris and get astride the River Seine by D + 90. That, then was the plan in bare outline. This is not the place to look at NEPTUNE, the operation designed to assemble, load, transport, protect and deliver the land force onto its objective, the north coast of France. Space precludes us from examining the beaches that stretch from east to west, SWORD, JUNO, GOLD and the beach furthest West, UTAH. It is that beach in the-middle, OMAHA, that attracts our attention.

Packed landing craft

Distribution of individual packed rations

Pointe du Hoc

OMAHA BEACH

A doomed site

So, what is OMAHA? OMAHA is a gently sloping beach on the north coast of Normandy that forms a shallow concave impression between long, hundred- foot high cliffs which run from Port en Bessin to Grandcamp Maisy. The beach itself, which is much the same as it was in 1944, is near to six thousand yards long and is almost devoid of natural obstacles. It is formed by a gentle slope of compacted sand, some three hundred yards in width (although this width is extended to almost seven hundred yards at a spring tide) across which runs an ever changing lattice of runnels, parallel to the shoreline, which at low tide are between eighteen inches and two-and-a-half feet deep. At the top of the beach is a band of shingle, a deep mass of multiple-sized, polished stones of varying colour which run almost the entire length of the shore. In 1944 this shingle bank was deeper and wider. Tailing down to the beach in steep, narrow valleys from the small rather unkempt road that runs between Arromanches, Port-en-Bessin, Grandcamp and Isigny were four unsurfaced tracks all of which were, at the time, wide enough for, say, a three ton truck, with the exception of the unsurfaced track from Vierville . These valleys cut through a bluff that lay behind the beach - a bluff that varied in height and steepness. To the west it was almost vertical in parts and to the east was more like a gently rolling slope. In both cases the Germans had moulded their defence into the sections of the slope that covered the four main exits. At the head of the tracks were the rather scattered farm-hamlets of Vierville to the west, St Laurent in the centre and Colleville to the east. These hamlets had sat on this rather unremarkable landscape for centuries. Architectural indifference combined with agricultural parsimony has even today failed to make them attractive. As a region, the hinterland was poor - a collection of small fields, unkempt hedges made more untidy by the total absence of farm workers to maintain them (they were in Germany as forced labour) and from place to place thick thorn hedgerows, up to eighteen feet wide that were to inflict such difficulty on the movement of infantry and tanks, enemy and Allies alike, later in the days and weeks after the landing. This, then, was the topographical background against which the Allies formed their plan.

The US Army combat uniform

German defences

German soldier arming an anti-personnel mine

Those troops that had successfully navigated the obstacles then had to cross a belt of shingle and what was effectively a narrow, flat shelf before climbing the bluffs. This shelf was well covered with mines of all types and, of course, barbed wire. Above the wire and either on top or near the top of the bluff were a succession of nests containing automatic weapons, placed in enfilade to make the most efficient killing ground on the beach. At either end of the crescent shaped beach were four massive concrete casements which held, mostly, a seventy five mm gun. All of these were of different origins. Now and again there were smaller and less obvious gun positions which contained anti-tank guns. Most nests had two mortar pits. Approximately seven hundred yards behind the position were 40 rocket pits each constructed to fire four 85 mm rockets. All of these weapons were sited in enfilade, along the beach. The machine guns, numbering about 120, were sited in cross-enfilade so that the beaten-zone of every gun crossed at more than one point. It was these machine guns and their beaten zones bisecting the beach that were to inflict such devastating casualties on the slow moving American soldiers.

German soldiers laying anti-tank mines

A mass-produced invitation to the Germans - surrender now and live in comfort and be well fed

Rommel inspecting the beach fortifications

DEUTSCHER SOLDAT!

Wir versprechen Dir kein Paradies, wenn Du gefangen wirst. Du kannst aber bestimmt auf das Folgende rechnen :

1. **ANSTÄNDIGE BEHANDLUNG,** wie sie einem tapferen Feind zusteht. Kriegsgefangene behalten Rang und Ehrenzeichen. Deine unmittelbaren Vorgesetzten sind Kameraden der Wehrmacht.

2. **GUTES ESSEN.** Als Kriegsgefangener bekommst Du dasselbe Essen wie unsere eignen Truppen.

3. **ERSTKLASSIGE KRANKENPFLEGE** für die Kranken und Verwundeten. Nach den Bestimmungen der Genfer Konvention erhalten Kriegsgefangene dieselbe Krankenpflege wie unsere eignen Truppen.

4. **POSTVERBINDUNG MIT DER HEIMAT.** Du kannst monatlich drei Briefe und vier Postkarten schreiben. Postverbindungen sind zuverlässig und verhältnismässig schnell. Du darfst auch selber Briefe und Pakete geschickt bekommen.

5. **BESOLDUNG.** Nach den Bestimmungen der Genfer Konvention haben auch Kriegsgefangene noch Anspruch auf ihre Besoldung. Für jede freiwillige Arbeitsleistung wirst Du extra bezahlt. Du hast auch das Recht, in den Lagerkantinen einzukaufen.

6. **BERUFSFORTBILDUNG.** Wenn Du es wünschst, wird Dir Gelegenheit zur Berufsfortbildung gegeben. Deutschland braucht nach dem Kriege gelernte Arbeiter.

Ihr werdet als Soldaten behandelt werden. Nach dem Kriege kommt Ihr selbstverständlich nach Hause

The German formations

The artillery was located approximately three miles inland in well-concealed positions invisible to the Americans and their support ships. It was thought at the time that the soldiers manning these weapons and defences came from the 716th Infantry Division which had, as its area of responsibility a position stretching between the Vire and the Orne rivers. There were two regiments in that division, one of which, the 726th Infantry Regiment was responsible for the area exclusive Grandcamp inclusive Port en Bessin. Most of the soldiers were not German – a roll call would have revealed a variety of nationalities, Volga Tartars, Uzbeks, Georgians, Armenians a few Poles and Czechs to name but a few. Sometimes it transpired that these few had no desire to die for Adolph Hitler. Behind the 726th was thought to be part of 352nd Infantry Division in the Saint Lo - Caumont area commanded by Lt Gen Heinz Hellmich. It was thought to be at full strength but was probably 30%

Rommel

down in numbers. Unknown to Gerow's staff, part of the 352nd Division in the shape of elements of 916 and 914 Regiment were up front, between Colleville and Isigny. Further east was a battalion located in the area of Ryes and Bayeux.

German rocket launcher and crew

1st Division shoulder flash

V Corps Plan

OMAHA was assigned to Leonard Gerow's V Corps. Its Headquarters began to participate in the planning for the forthcoming assault on northern France in July 1943. By October, the headquarters of 1 US Army had established themselves in England and were able to guide, take an interest in and interchange views with V Corps. What is referred to as 'this interchange of views' included of course constant communication with the navy and the air force. The whole being welded together between January to May 1944, V Corps Plan being produced on 26th March. The complicated loading plan and troop lists were omitted and only began to be implemented by the end of May. Naturally the overall plan and the detailed movement and logistic plans had to be tested against reality in the months during planning and for this purpose the training areas of Ilfracombe Beach in North Devonshire and Slapton Sands in South Devonshire were used as assault training areas with Dartmouth being used as a centre, or proving ground, of

joint army/navy planning. Exercise DUCK in January 1944, besides being a form of dress-rehearsal led the planners to believe, for instance, that a force of three divisions could be despatched from Plymouth and Falmouth instead of the one division originally envisaged. Training and planning seemed to go hand in hand. Exercise followed exercise. Plans were changed or adjusted and the final revision of the NEPTUNE printed. This was a document of 326 foolscap pages with 23 maps and charts. The complexity and magnitude of the invasion force as it was to approach Omaha is well illustrated by the numbers of ships of all sizes. For instance O Force required 7 transports, 8 LSIs, 24 LSTs. 33 LCIs, 36 LCMs, 147 LCTs and over 33 other craft in addition to the escort ships.

29th Division training on Dartmoor

Washing kit and razor, etc

Gerow

Leaving aside the actual hour of invasion and the arguments over whether it was to be in darkness or daylight, the actual choice for the day of the landing, D-Day, was governed by a variety of factors. It was better for the moon to be full for the easier night-landing of parachute troops on the two flanks. A full moon would also aid the handling of the multitude of ships steaming cross-channel. There was a requirement for the landing craft, of all sizes, to be near the off loading point about an hour after first light so that the seaborne order for assault could be adjusted ship-by-ship off shore. The dawn light would also help accurate, preparatory bombardment but Gerow and Huebner, GOC 1 US Div, felt that this naval gunfire would be too light and too short and made their objections felt. The last absolute requirement was that the tide on landing should be 2 hours before high water at H Hr.

A few magazines

Only certain dates conformed to these imperatives, 21/23 May, 5/7 June and 19/21 June. On the 8th May D-Day was fixed for 5th June but on the 3rd June the Meteorological staff gave Eisenhower an unfavourable forecast for the 5th predicting overcast skies and a strong wind with heavy seas. At 0415hrs on 4th June he decided to postpone D-Day for 24 hrs. A division, which had already set sail, was recalled! Conditions on the 6th June were forecast to be slightly better and at 0415 hrs on the 5th of June Eisenhower decided to go.

The ultimate objectives of V Corps

In 1944 the *Mission* was normally referred to as the *Aim*. For V Corps this was to secure a bridgehead between Port-en-Bessin and the Vire River from which they could debouch towards Caumont and Saint Lô conforming with the right flank of the Second British Army. The Corps planned to arrive on the beach in four stages, 1 US Division and 29 US Division leading. The former had seen service in North Africa and Sicily, the latter were about to see their first fighting in Normandy. The initial assault was to be under the command of the GOC 1 US Division with elements of 29 US Division. This was termed FORCE 'O'. Second was the follow up (FORCE 'B') which would begin landing during the afternoon of D-Day.

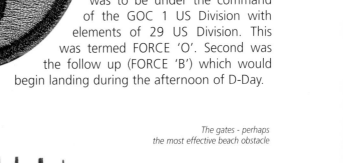

29th Division shoulder flash

The gates - perhaps the most effective beach obstacle

Supporting fire from USS Arkansas

Gunfire - USS Nevada

Third was the arrival of the main body of the reserve division, 2 US Division during D+1 and D+ 2. Fourth was the arrival of what are know as Corps Troops who would be landed between D+3 and D+15. The loading priorities at the departure ports were such that they mirrored this intention. FORCE 'O' numbered 34,142 men and 3,306 vehicles. Slightly smaller was FORCE 'B' which numbered 25,117 men and 4,429 vehicles. The remaining forces numbered about 49,000 troops and almost 10,000 vehicles but many of these were not part of the V Corps order of battle. V Corps had to face Germans who had positioned themselves with everything in the shop-window. OMAHA Beach was well obstructed by a variety of structures, the most formidable of which was a gate with girder supports some ten feet high, the whole liberally covered with Teller mines. Log fascines, again liberally covered with mines, were interspersed whilst, nearer the shore, say 150 yards below the low water mark, were steel girders, in threes,

Some reading

*The Stars and Stripes newspaper
the army's daily broadsheet*

crossed at the centre with sharpened ends capable of opening up a landing craft like a tin-opener. Although these obstacles were not in continuous lines the gaps were sometimes partially filled with concrete triangles, some with a mine on the top spigot. Today they form a harmless tourist attraction at the water's edge.

Before the assault, an intensive air and ship-to-shore bombardment was planned. 480 B-24s were to attack various target areas in the V Corps Zone with 1285 tons of fragmentation and high explosive bombs, both with instantaneous fuzes to avoid cratering. The Navy were to commence ship to shore bombardment forty minutes before H Hr stopping at H- 3 minutes. *USS Texas* and *Arkansas* planned to concentrate on Pointe du Hoc and Exit D-3 and three cruisers planned to concentrate on the D-3 and E-1 exits and targets to either flank of the invasion beach. Nearer inshore were eight destroyers who planned to take on individual beach strongpoints.

For close protection there were in addition 33 mine sweepers and four other destroyers. The naval task force was completed by 105 other ships and 585 vessels used for service work. On landing it was planned that forward observation officers (FOOs), one assigned to every battalion, would direct fire further inshore.

The beach was divided into two sections. 1 US Division to the left and 29 US Division to the right. 1 US Division had served in North Africa and Sicily and was battle-hardened whereas 29 US Div, a National Guard Division from Virginia and Maryland, had had no battle experience – although well-trained on Dartmoor and Exmoor.

The infantryman's rifle

Omaha sector

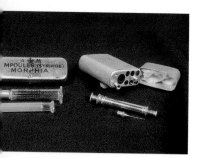

Morphine pack

TNT explosive pack

The infantryman's comb

The assault was to be made with one Regimental Combat Team (equivalent to the fighting elements of a British brigade) on either side of the half way mark along a line running from St Laurent to Formigny and on to the Aure river. On the right was 116 RCT, which would attack on DOG GREEN, DOG WHITE, DOG RED and EASY GREEN. On the left was 16 RCT which was to land on EASY RED and FOX GREEN. 116 RCT was to deploy one Ranger Company and two battalion landing teams in the initial assault, leaving the third battalion landing team in reserve, afloat. It was also given two Ranger battalions for the capture of Pointe du Hoc. The battalion objectives, common to both RCTs, were firstly the Beachead Maintenance Line (a few hundred yards inland) and ultimately, at the end of the day, the D-Day Phase line (along a line Isigny-Canchy-Trevieres). The objective of 116 RCT was to capture Vierville, Pointe du Hoc, Grandcamp and Isigny including an area up to the Vire river. The 1st Battalion was to land on DOG GREEN with its five companies in column including a company from the Ranger Battalion. The 2nd Battalion 116 RCT was to land on DOG WHITE DOG RED and EASY GREEN with three companies abreast. The 3rd Battalion, in reserve, was to land behind the 2nd Battalion on DOG WHITE, DOG RED and EASY GREEN. Over on the left, the 16th RCT was to land on EASY RED and FOX GREEN with two battalions abreast. On EASY RED, the 2nd Battalion was to land with two companies leading, abreast with the aim of capturing Colleville and the high ground to the south. The 3rd Battalion was to land on FOX GREEN with two companies up and two in reserve and head towards St Honorine and link up with 50th Division. The 1st Battalion was to be afloat, in reserve.

Webbing tie for equipment

Standard issue gas-mask

The timing of the assault was to be two hours before high water and as dawn was breaking – this was H-Hr. At five minutes before H-Hr B and C Companies of 743 Tank Battalion would emerge from the waves onto the beach, having swum in from 5000 yards offshore, at DOG WHITE and DOG GREEN and take up fire-support positions. When the tide rose it was planned that the tanks would help clear exit D-3. A Company of the tank battalion was to follow in eight LCTs and land on EASY GREEN and DOG RED at H-Hr together with a miscellany of armoured engineer equipment including dozer tanks for the demolition of obstacles. This force as a whole, it was hoped, would engage the enemy defensive positions and cover the work of the 146 Engineer Combat Battalion which was given the task of clearing and marking eight lanes through the beach obstacles. They planned to land at H+3 to H+8 minutes. The inward tidal movement of approximately eighty yards an hour gave them about 22 minutes to achieve this job. It was planned that the artillery support, led by 58 Armoured Artillery Battalion, would land between H+90 and H+120 minutes. On the eastern side of the beach elements of 1 Division would land in a pattern that was almost identical.

COVER. WATERPROOF. RIFLE
SPEC P O D No. 377
STOCK NO 74-C-310 -41
ORDER DATED JULY 27 1943
PHILADELPHIA Q.M. DEPOT
PURCH. ORDER 573

Waterproof rifle cover

The plans were flawed – too few infantry units were spread over over too wide an area and no notice at all had been taken of experience gained with great loss of life in the Pacific and Mediterranean. The ideal attainment was to break through the enemy defences within two hours of landing and clear the exits by H+3hrs. At this point the companies were to re-group and re-form battalion groups. The whole thrust, if it went to plan would drive the enemy from the hinterland south to Cerisy la Foret, west to the Vire River and east to near Port en Bessin. Enough space, just, to accept the reinforcements, to build up reserves quicker than the enemy and to house supplies for onwards operations.

View of the assault from USS Ancona

Combat engineers arrive on beach

THE ATTACK

Before daybreak

In the week of 26th May the entire invasion force began its move to the sealed camps on the edge of their respective embarkation areas. Up until this time only the individual Commanding Officers of the invasion battalions had been informed of their own detailed plan - now they were able, in the sealed camp, to pass on this knowledge to their company commanders and they, in turn passed on their orders to their young officers and NCOs. Place names were replaced by code-words and were only identified when the troops were on board ship. At dawn on 5th June the first ships began their voyage and by midday some 1200 warships and 4128 Landing Craft had set sail. In mid channel minesweepers had carefully swept an area where the armada met - called Picadilly Circus - and from there the five landing groups set out on an exact bearing to their respective beach in a difficult Atlantic swell that was barely mitigated by the Cotentin Peninsula.

Touchdown 0630hrs

In the half-light of a rough and windy Normandy morning, the first tanks of B and C Companies 741 Tank Battalion were launched from their mother-ship at H-50 some 6000 yards offshore.

Landing craft 400 metres off shore

Within a minute or so the canvas sides that formed a bulwark around the upper part of every tank collapsed under pressure from the waves. 32 tanks were launched. 25 sank, leaving only a few of their crews, swimming or on rafts in the rough water, awaiting rescue. Only 2 tanks arrived on the beach at the east end of EASY RED. A short time later 3 other tanks were landed on the beach by an LCT that could not open its ramp at sea. Within ten minutes all 5 tanks were out of action. On the Western side of the beach common sense prevailed and the commanders of the LCTs carried the 743rd Tank battalion onto the beach, but not without casualties. Many of the officers had been killed or wounded during the hour before touch-down and many of the tanks were unserviceable. Of the battalion's 32 tanks that arrived 8 out of 16 were fit for combat from B Company and these took up positions immediately to help the infantry on the area of beach around DOG GREEN and DOG WHITE.

The tanks of A and C Companies touched down at intervals slightly to the east, without loss. The delay imposed by rough weather had the effect of confusing the careful time-table for the landings. The infantry had been offloaded onto their tiny landing craft, well out of the range of enemy artillery, nine miles out some twenty minutes early due to the sea-state. But even with this time-bonus most arrived on the beach late. Of, say, the 200 craft used for the initial landing only 10 are known to have been swamped but nearly all the passengers were rescued. The men who had fallen into the water whilst in transit were rescued later. Almost all of those who rea-

The second wave moves in

LCI 412 about to offload

ched the offloading point near the beach were wet, cold and seasick and were thus not in the best condition for an assault landing. Their difficulties were compounded by the fact that little notice had been taken of the very obvious rip-tide that runs along the beach and no notice had been taken at all of the runnels aforementioned. Thus not only did the flat-bottomed landing craft, devoid of a keel which prevents side-ways movement, all drift towards the east, some by distances up to a thousand yards, but some of those men who did land, in the sea-state of over three and a half feet high, found that the addition of a two foot runnel was too much to cope with.

Also, when encountering the statistical rogue wave of five feet, they drowned, unable to swim with the 70-pound load, on average, that they were carrying. In retrospect this gap in information during the planning stage, elementary for any person with experience of the sea, was more than remarkable and could almost be called reprehensible.

The effect of this drift, this rip, was to place sections and platoons in unfamiliar positions and in almost all cases these same detachments became mixed up with other formations, isolated from their unit commanders, and, worse, from their planned minor objectives, in a ghastly muddle. A muddle of merely eight infantry companies was, with hindsight, too small a force to cover in any way a beach of almost 6000 yards and it was this inadequate force that very nearly lost the battle as a whole on OMAHA, however valiantly they fought. It was as if a ball of string was unravelling. One mistake in planning seemed to pile on others, on and on as this account will show. This is not a criticism of the fighting, it is a statement referring to planning, the details of which were insufficiently thought out. The Germans, all along the beach, had precise orders not to open fire on their enemies, if they landed, until all had disembarked from the landing craft. Naturally, young officers were first out along side their signaller. Both were the first to be killed or wounded. Those infantrymen who followed soon became casualties and by the time that the average platoon had reached the cover of the sea-wall or the shingle to the east only 40% were still alive, often leaderless and almost all without any form of wireless communication, a line of wet khaki. They had been brought to the beach in boat sections six to a company, every boat carrying an average of 31 men including an officer or sergeant The Headquarters section was carried in the second wave. Loading had been meticulous – the first to land was either the young officer or the section leader with five men armed with M-1s, everybody carrying 96 rounds of ammunition. A wire-cutting team followed. Next out were the BAR teams of two men each carrying 900 rounds per gun, 2 bazooka teams, a 60-mm mortar team with 20 rounds, a flame thrower team and finally a demolition team with bangalore torpedoes and pack-charges of TNT. On some boats two medical personnel brought up the rear. All soldiers wore drab uniform impregnated with a chemical to protect against gas.

Soldiers from 5 Engineer Special Brigade come ashore

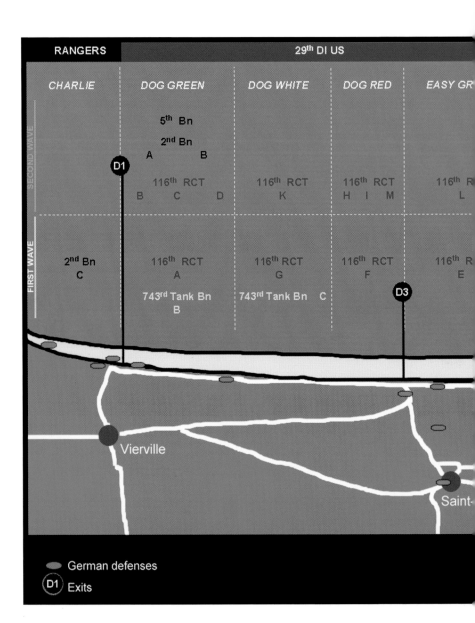

RANGERS | 29th DI US

CHARLIE | DOG GREEN | DOG WHITE | DOG RED | EASY GR

SECOND WAVE

5th Bn

2nd Bn
A   B

D1

116th RCT
B   C   D

116th RCT
K

116th RCT
H   I   M

116th R
L

FIRST WAVE

2nd Bn
C

116th RCT
A

116th RCT
G

116th RCT
F

116th R
E

743rd Tank Bn
B

743rd Tank Bn   C

D3

Vierville

Saint-

German defenses

D1 Exits

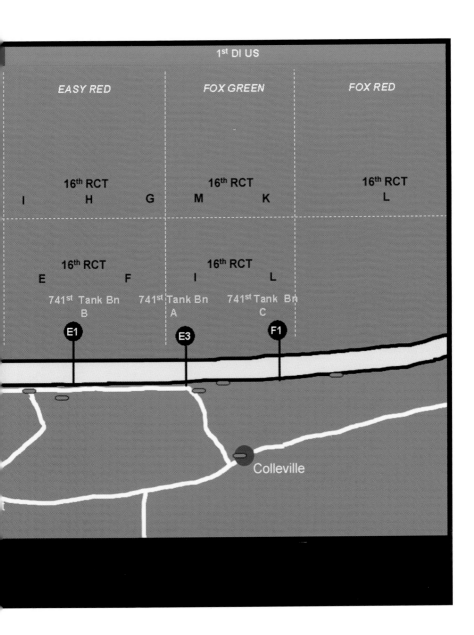

Climbing rope and ladder

Pointe du Hoc

"O" Force was responsible for Pointe du Hoc some six miles to the west. Four companies of the 2nd Ranger Battalion under their Commanding Officer, Lt. Col James Rudder, who became Principal of Texas A&M after the war, had been given the task of assaulting the position. The aim was to eliminate six 155-mm guns of the 1260 Arty Regiment and 125 soldiers from 726 Infantry Regiment. These guns had a range of approximately thirteen miles and were well within range of the shipping at Utah Beach and all the

landing area of Omaha, including the trans-shipping position ten miles out. The Rangers had disembarked into their British LCAs that morning at 4 am from the cross-channel steamer, *Amsterdam*, and headed directly for their objective becoming, on the way, passive spectators of the main landing at Omaha. The leading boat had to be bailed out by pumps and helmets, but survived. A navigation mistake almost put some of the landing craft onto a similar headland, causing a delay of about thirty minutes. Eventually D, E and F companies made contact with what was in effect the advance party, a section of C Company, and landed in their midst rather than wasting time heading for the western side of the objective.

Lt. Col James Rudder at Pointe du Hoc

Ropes attached to grapnels were fired into the cliff top by rocket guns and the tubular-steel ladders, provided by the London Fire Brigade, were swiftly set up alongside over the slimy sandstone cliff edge. Up the Rangers went in spite of interference from the German garrison who, having survived the bombing and the shelling from USS Texas, were still fighting. The Rangers charged through, driving the enemy before them over the main road and some four hundred yards to the South where they proceeded to dig in, deny the main road to the enemy and repel the expected counter-attack. The guns were not in place and for some reason, unknown to this day, the Germans had replaced them with telegraph poles surmounted by camouflage nets. A fighting patrol found the guns almost by mistake that afternoon, some 700 yards inland and disabled them with a grenade in every breach-block. Back in the main position a small party had tried to take on the anti-aircraft gun position (which still exists to the West) but had failed due to the Germans' skilful use of the communication trenches.

Two assaults were made and both sadly failed. Further forward Rudder was driven back by the inevitable enemy counter attack. It was fortunate that although Rudder was out of communication with the beach at Omaha, he was in contact with some of the support ships by wireless and light-signal. *USS Satterlee*, now on her own after the departure back to Portsmouth of *HMS Talybont* which had been damaged by an enemy shell, stayed on station and provided valuable fire and communication support. Conditions for Rudder's force had become critical overnight after another German attack had almost cut his small perimeter in half. By now he had a mere 90 men left out of the original 210 and they had no water, no food, no ammunition and practically no medical supplies. For weapons, they had seized abandoned German rifles and light machine guns and for support they relied on the accurate fire of Destroyers *Thompson, Barton, Harding and O'Brien*. On 7th June a relieving force attempted to make contact with Rudder's men but had to halt because of sustained artillery and small arms fire a few hundred yards from their comrades forward positions. At the same time, two LCPVs landed at the base of the cliff with 30 reinforcements and much needed food, water and ammunition. All this took the pressure off Rudder but he was still in an

unenviable position. It was not until the following afternoon that at last, part of the 5th Rangers and the 1st Battalion of the 116th succeeded, by cross country march in joining up with Rudder's men supported by about 140 rounds from the *USS Ellyson*. However tragedy struck at the final moment – Rudder's men were firing captured German weapons: the friendly tanks identified the muzzle signature putting in rapid fire. Twenty Rangers were killed. The Pointe du Hoc was cleared.

Cliff-side command post
Pointe du Hoc

Kirk and Bradley watch landing from USS Augusta

The second wave - 0700 hrs

Back at OMAHA, on D-Day, the second wave, the Special Engineer Task Force, manned by the Navy and the Army, suffered a similar fate to the first wave. Here again the planning was ill thought out. The rip-tide threw most of the engineer effort off-course, leaving the 29 Division sector virtually uncovered. At least three engineer teams set themselves up where no infantry or tank fire-cover was available. Insufficient thought was given to the speed of the incoming tide, eighty yards an hour. Thus, even without enemy action, the half hour allotted to them for clearing obstacles and setting up cleared corridors was insufficient. Over half of the engineer teams were ten minutes late in arriving and this compounded the problem. Those engineers that did valiantly carry on, too few to have very much effect, were excellent targets for enemy fire and their pre-loaded inflatable boats were vulnerable to every chance shot or piece of shrapnel. Most of their kit was, consequently, lost. Their work was severely hampered by infantry who were late in landing and by the second wave of assault troops, some of whom attempted to take cover behind those obstacles that offered a chance of survival. This was truly a chapter lifted

Newspaper headline

ES ARMEES ALLIEES DEBARQUENT

out of Dante's Inferno, a seemingly endless number of casualties, all caused by accurate shell-fire from artillery behind the beach. This shell-fire was not effective on the wet sand but, in amongst the landing craft and the engineer parties, it was lethal and the casualties piled up and up. By the time the engineers were no longer able to work because of the speed of the rising tide six gaps had been cleared along the 6000 yard beach – four on EASY RED and the other two around DOG WHITE, but they had only been able to mark one of these gaps.

The worst of the underwater obstacles - sharp at all ends, it could rip open a landing-craft

Accepting that the shell-fire was more than effective among the landing craft and the obstacles, it was the uncovered sand that formed the killing ground so effectively covered by the enemy machine guns. These were organised into some eight nests of approximately ten medium machine-guns each with a mortar section and in most cases either two anti-tank guns or howitzers of various calibres and makes. The casualties on this killing ground were such that the assault almost had to be abandoned and the remnants evacuated. To this day, too little attention is paid to the effect of the interconnected beaten zones of the enemy automatic-weapon defence.

The assault goes in

DUKWs bring in supplies - but not enough

The beaten zones were so arranged that any invader would have to get through several, crossing, sometimes interconnecting areas of shot-fall. This shot-fall, normally only adjusted by a notch or two, approximately one or two degrees, covered an area some 100 yards long by one yard wide at a rate of 1,200 rounds a minute. The beaten zone was fixed, a happening that was discovered and taken advantage of by invading infantrymen later in the day. It was, thus, this criss-cross of beaten zones and the hazard of the two to three foot runnels in the sand, below the waterline, that inflicted such heavy casualties on the American troops.

LCI 553 and 410 landing troops

US Coastguard rescue boat

Hell on the Beach

In terms of effectiveness, the beaten zones were at their worst opposite Vierville, DOG GREEN and DOG WHITE. A Company of the 116th was to land at DOG GREEN with C Company of the 2nd Battalion of the Rangers. Here the rip-tide was less effective in pushing the landing craft off course because of the slight promontory to the west. Offshore, one of the six LCAs foundered. Of the men who jumped overboard almost all drowned immediately, dragged down by their heavy equipment. At about H+6 minutes the landing craft that remained grounded about 30 yards on the seaward side of some of the obstacles in about four ft of water. The infantry quickly disembarked in three files, in good order. Almost immediately the enemy automatic fire from light machine guns was brought to bear, every shot fired to kill and aimed accordingly. A series of mortar Bombs destroyed one landing craft sending shrapnel and lethal debris over a wide area, killing and wounding troops in the water. On one boat all the men jumped into the water and died by drowning in the depths of a deep runnel. Those who arrived on the sand were then hit whilst crossing the beaten zones. Few survived. Every officer was a casualty and most of the sergeants were killed or wounded. Fifteen minutes after landing A Company had sustained casualties amounting to 75% together with all its junior leaders and officers. Most of the company who survived were dead within hours due to an inability to get to the dry land protected by an almost unscaleable sea-wall.

They drowned. The Ranger Company alongside A Company, in two LCAs (there were 65 men to a Ranger Company) motored in at H+15 and suffered similarly. Few made the shore, just 30 men survived. B Company, following, suffered a similar fate to A and became an almost total loss.

G Company on the flank of A was meant to land alongside but drifted over a thousand yards to the east. Here, widely separated by the effects of the current, some had a relatively unscathed landing, but on EASY GREEN the part of G Company which had drifted there walked into severe enemy fire and lost up to 60% of its men. Taking cover by the sea wall they understandably lost momentum and huddled there uncertain of where to go and what to do. F Company suffered a similar fate when they landed opposite the Les Moulins hamlet at EASY GREEN and lost 50% of their number by the time they reached the sea wall that, here, was only a third of the height of its continuation at Vierville. E Company drifted well over the inter-division boundary and landed in widely separated sections well into EASY RED. Here the runnels took over from the Germans in exacting casualties. Many men tried to swim but were drowned. Those who did manage to wade or successfully swim lost most of their equipment but by the time they reached the sea wall the large majority of those who had not drowned had been wounded.

Hell on the beach
logs and steel obstacles

Casualty on the shingle

Help at hand on the beach - NB the blood plasma

The wreckage burns

Perhaps FOX GREEN was the worst section of beach. Here, on the western side of FOX GREEN, E Company of 16th RCT landed and ran into particularly effective beaten zones resulting in 95% casualties. F Company landed on the east side of EASY RED, the current dispersing the platoons over one thousand yards. Two officers survived. The Company suffered 60% casualties. The remainder of the battalion, I and L Companies, were delayed in transit from the mother-craft. I Company had two craft swamped whilst the others drifted almost towards Port en Bessin. L Company arrived off the beach some 30 minutes late but found that their section of FOX GREEN was almost under the cover of a miniature cliff. In this safe ground the platoons were able to organise themselves and became the only Company in good enough shape to carry out their particular mission.

If that was the account of the first and second waves, the third wave was much the same. There was no safe ground to advance to, just a collection of survivors along the sea-wall and the shingle. The engineers were still hampered by delayed or lost landing craft later in the day and were unable to work to full efficiency. In the 116th area the casualties were as heavy as those within the first wave and the scattering of sections and platoons was just as serious. However C Company of the 116th landed on DOG WHITE in error and with the exception of one landing craft, landed together. There was a mishap when one of the craft overturned in the heavy surf, swamping the flame-throwers and the heavy weapons but the German fire was much lighter than before and their aim had been disturbed due to undergrowth fires probably started by the phosphorous smoke shells fired by a destroyer on the right flank.

Dead soldiers

The Company swiftly reorganised itself and was in relatively good order. D Company was the victim of bad seamanship – three of its landing craft were swamped, many drowned and those that did land had great difficulty getting to the sea-wall. Headquarter Company was brought in under the cliffs at DOG GREN but lost over 50% including the Commanding Officer of the Artillery Battalion. For almost the whole day they were held down by particularly accurate sniper and small-arms fire. H Company of 2nd BLT arrived at about 0730 hrs but were unable to give any adequate supporting fire. Battalion HQ and Headquarters Company came in on DOG RED just after 0700 hrs but sustained heavy casualties from accurate German fire. The Commanding Officer, Major Sidney Bingham, was amongst the first to reach the shingle line but having no wireless communication he had great difficulty commanding his scattered Companies and part of F Company that had arrived on the shingle with him. He did manage to coerce about fifty men to assault a three storey house at Les Moulins and advance up to the top of the bluff of the D-3 draw.

Death next to a pointed log

However their weapons were clogged with sand and water, their volume of fire almost miniscule and they had to retreat back to the house.

Part of G Company had landed in the wrong position but gradually worked their way Westwards losing any form of cohesion the further they marched. 3 BLT of the 116th was due to land behind 2 BLT at about 0730 hrs on DOG WHITE and DOG RED and this they managed to do without heavy casualties but the platoons were mixed up and the beach overcrowded. They sank down by the sea wall exhausted and there they stayed. It was at the end of the third wave that the 116th command group arrived in the persons of Colonel Charles Canham and Brigadier General Norman Cota. Avoiding an obstacle on DOG WHITE and just missing a Teller mine in the water, they landed amongst some of the C Company men and elements of the 2nd Battalion shrouded by the smoke already mentioned. The landing and the timing were fortuitous.

German prisoners load their wounded onto LCIs for transport to a hospital ship

Beach-master's command post

The first incursions inland

Norman Cota was one of America's most distinguished soldiers and that June morning it might have appeared to anybody who could spare a thought, that the Almighty cared for him. He walked up and down, up and down in the maelstrom of the automatic-weapon-covered beach, urging his men on and up the bluffs in front of them. Nobody moved. Eventually after half an hour Cota said to those who could listen "all right, I am going…" with a few expletives added. Followed by about seventy men, who he shamed into following him, he went up a small valley on the other side of the coast road. The ground is such, west of Les Moulins, that the folds and small bushes give just about adequate cover – and this he took. Behind him the vehicles of the regiment had just begun to arrive on the slowly vanishing beach. Those that were not disabled by damp and salt water were caught in a traffic jam resembling a car park. Not much moved: the enemy had an easy target shoot. The losses of equipment were almost phenomenal – for instance the 397 Anti Aircraft Battalion lost 28 of its 36 machine guns and the infantry units had great difficulty if getting their heavy weapons ashore. The platoon and company wirelesses were almost completely disabled. None seemed to work. This of course had a deleterious effect on communication and command all day. There is no doubt, however sketchy the official records are, that morale on the beach slumped.

But there was some glimmer of hope for the invaders because, at several points along what seemed a hostile anonymous green bluff, there were minor penetrations that took advantage of the smoke from the burning undergrowth (obviously started by phosphorous smoke shells) or gunfire

The beach p.m.

from the few tanks bolstered by the odd salvo from out to sea. Perhaps C Company, backed up by Rangers from the 5th Battalion, made the most notable incursion, ably led by Norman Cota who led the initial crossing of the sea road. The small bare valley which he took is now marked by a form of junction-box on a telegraph pole and leads to the top of the bluff, from where it is comparatively easy to turn left or right towards St Laurent or Vierville. To the east Captain Norman Dawson with just one man as escort found his way almost to the top of the bluff where there was just one enemy machine gun. Stalking it he attacked it from behind and with one fragmentation grenade killed all the crew. His escort then descended the hill and collected the remains of G Company of the 116th who came up in bits having crossed the minefield on the level ground by the beach. The ground that this action was fought over is easily seen from the Observation Platform of the US Cemetery, looking east for about fifty yards. This small valley formed a funnel for ascent during the remainder of the morning.

Overall, by 0800hrs the other German nests covering the exits were still in action, the worst being the D3 and E3 defences. Assault groups had in some cases gone past these defences but were unsupported due to the engineers being unable to clear the beach and the flat ground immediately in front. The beach was getting smaller and smaller and vehicles were parked almost touching in some sections. Landing craft were vainly hunting for a vacant part of the sand to drop their ramps on. Perhaps Cannon Company of 16 RCT was a good illustration – they landed their half tracks at 0830hrs after two attempts but could not move through the litter of disabled vehicles. However conditions improved later in the morning when some movement was possible as the enemy guns ' rate of fire diminished. We can leave the beach at this point with the view of one of the tanks from 741 Tank Battalion standing on the beach firing at the enemy until the water finally rose over the gun barrel and LCT 30 with LCI 544 ramming through the beach obstacles with all guns firing at enemy emplacements.

The artificial harbour begins to be laid down

These isolated actions were not wholly what they seemed in writing – many more similar actions were taking place along the 6,000 yards front which, together, helped in weakening the German resistance. By 1,100 or just afterwards this resistance was noticeably much less. Only comparatively recently has evidence been produced that the enemy was in fact running out of ammunition – a weakness so elementary that it barely seems believable. But true it was. Perhaps the decisive improvement along this ghastly beach came at the E 1 draw when E Company of 16th Infantry Battalion partially neutralised the eastern side of the German defences, aided by M Company of 116 Infantry Battalion on the west which was taking on an unfinished German defensive position still in action.

At the same time the engineers from 37th Engineer Combat Battalion were able to bulldoze a wide gap through the sand dunes to the East and men of 149 Engineer Combat Battalion made anther gap to the west. 18th RCT had been scheduled to land on Omaha at about 0930hrs but, delayed by the congestion on the beach, were over half an hour late. However very few men became casualties on landing. On the right of the E 1 draw the 2nd Battalion found a strongpoint still in action. Fire from a nearby tank was not enough to help the battalion forward and the attack stalled. A Naval Gunfire Support Team, fortunately nearby, directed the guns of a destroyer 1,000 yards offshore on a successful shoot of four rounds: the enemy surrendered.

This small action was one of the rare times that communication shore-to-ship worked. On the Command net, i.e. from Division to, say, Regiment it was virtually non existent. Thus the E 1 draw was now ostensibly open and ready to become the main funnel for movement off the beach after half an hours work by the 16 RCT Engineers to clear it of mines. This however sounds all too neat and easy – it was not. Congestion slowed everything down and an incorrect landfall, almost an hour too early, by the forward units of 115th Infantry, who should have been some 1,000 yards to the West, caused further confusion for both regiments which was not sorted out until about 0100hrs. It was fortunate that the shot-fall of the enemy mortar fire was ineffective. Perhaps more fortunate, the German artillery forward observation officers could not direct fire accurately.

Moving off the beach
1st Division sector

Apple orchard beyond the beach - NB the obscured views

Taking the coastline villages

Put in a nutshell, there had been limited advances up the bluffs until about 1030hrs but further forceful advance by the invading forces was stopped not only by the congestion and confusion on an ever-shrinking beach, but also by the firm control that minor German units had of the countryside on top of the bluffs. In general the exits led to three villages and it was the action in and around these villages that delayed V Corps very far short of its D-Day objectives. At Vierville C Company of the 1st Battalion led the way up a small indentation near le Hamel followed closely by eight companies of the Rangers, some engineers from 121 Engineer Combat Battalion and fragments of B, F, G and H Companies. The Command element of 116 RCT had arrived on the top of the bluff at about 0915hrs. They found almost complete confusion. Few wirelesses worked, probably due to sea water and damage. Units had become intermingled and the multi-unit force was spread over a number of unconnected fields with thick, high hedges that prevented observation. The Regimental Commander, Colonel Canham, was thus, isolated, not knowing where his subordinates were and out of communication from the beach. Brigadier General Norman Cota, who had landed earlier, with the second infantry wave at about 0830hrs had led a charmed life on the beach urging anybody who would listen to get up the bluffs to no avail. It was he who ultimately led this somewhat unmanageable collection of soldiers up the minor valley. He had directed the Ranger element south of Vierville and the elements of 116th towards the village itself. The Rangers attack petered out in front of heavy resistance but Norman Cota's force from the 116th arrived in the village at about 1,100 and secured some of the houses. C Company with B Company of the 5th Rangers now decided to push forward towards Pointe du Hoc but were too weak to make progress. The main Ranger Battalion then moved in to help them but were called off by Colonel Canham who needed them to defend Vierville that evening and night. Thus at dusk the Regimental Commander was in a position, south of Vierville, that should normally have been occupied by an infantry platoon. One of his battalions was in the Vierville area and two of his battalions around St Laurent to the east. The Vierville draw was open, just but no reinforcements had been landed and none had wended their way up the valley which had been cleared since USS Texas had bombarded the enemy strong-points around the draw. Shortly after 1pm Norman Cota, escorted by five men and driving some prisoners in front of them had gone down the valley to find out why no traffic of any kind had come through. He discovered a few survivors of A Company 116th and a small group of engineers from the 121st Engineer Group who had apparently lost 75% of their equipment on landing, scattered between the D 1 and D 3 draws.

The thick bocage that was unexpected - NB the unkempt hedge after 4 years of neglect

The picture at St Laurent was not different. The high ground had been reached by a mixed company from 116th Infantry at about 1000 but little progress was made for the rest of the day in the confused fighting that took place. The enemy had the advantage of good fields of fire due to the comparatively open country just north of the village towards the E 1 Draw and in particular an enemy company was in control of the area west of the village all afternoon. At dusk the greater part of the 3rd Battalion was still near the top of the draw and just part of two companies of the 2nd Battalion, G and F, were nearby with Battalion HQ. The 115 Infantry had landed just in front of the E 1 draw at noon but, hampered by a lack of battalion transport, its heavy weapons had to be man-handled up the draw. Hence, in an area of about one square mile the elements of five battalions fought their brave but unconnected battles with a scattered enemy.

Over at Colleville, earlier in the day, G Company had worked its way up the bluff and after clearing-out the enemy to the east of the village, became stuck on its eastern edge. On its way up it had collected elements from F Company and surprisingly a few sections from E Company of the 116th. During the unsuccessful move into the eastern part of the village these elements, through misunderstanding, had worked their way back towards the East and had become firmly held down by the enemy, who had regained the small area from which they had been driven earlier, an action that perhaps was the only enemy counter-attack that day. Isolated and held down at the east of the village G Company suffered twelve casualties from friendly ship-to-shore fire. Their isolation was only apparent. Nearby, to the West, groups of American infantry from a number of battalions were systematically trying to clear the enemy from the top of he bluff, but, hampered by the close, high hedges they were unable to see what was happening on their flanks and seemed to be fighting isolated uncoordinated battles with varying degrees of success. Varying because the Germans were also under the same conditions and, whilst holding the line in parts, were also trying to move back to better defensive positions sometimes on the coat-tails of the nearest American unit, to the utter confusion of both. The confusion on the high ground was reinforced by part of 18 RCT who had been diverted up the E 1 draw by Brigadier Wyman to push through the part of 16 RCT that was attempting to envelop Collevillle. However the cumulative resistance of small parties of well-led enemy infantry delayed their advance forward and it was not until midnight that Colleville village was finally captured. But even then part of the 3rd Battalion of 18 RCT was still north of the main road. Colleville was an example of heavy fighting and battlefield isolation due, mainly to the close terrain. The area of the bluff and fields north of Cabourg presented another example of this isolation. Here, the far left hand company of the 16 RCT suffered the same fate, on landing, as its neighbours, some 50% casualties. Nevertheless, on its own, the remainder of the company worked its way up the bluffs through a sharply indented valley now known as the F 1 draw and reached the top almost unscathed.

Vierville - pre-war

On its way up it collected two bulldozers from the traffic jam on the beach and, pushing them forward as it advanced, the company made an extra highway, which was rapidly used to thin-out those vehicles which were mobile and stranded on the sand. A vehicle park was made in a long field at the top of the new exit road. That done, Jimmy Monteith, the young officer in command – the remainder of the officers had become casualties on the beach – led his force into an attack on the enemy nest overlooking the eastern side of the beach, killing most of the occupants. Sadly this young man was himself killed by a stray bullet. He was later awarded the Congressional Medal of Honour and now lies in the St Laurent American Cemetery. Late that afternoon after tidy-up work by 336 Engineer Battalion, who had been moved over the entire length of the beach from Vierville, elements of 745 Tank Battalion were pushed up the new highway.

During this time the Destroyers continued their work of demolishing strong-points along the bluff. The Vierville nests as a whole were silenced by about 1300hrs but although the draw was now open there was not

enough infantry in that area of beach to mop-up the remaining, weakened enemy positions. These were quickly taken over again through the Germans' ability to move rapidly down previously evacuated communication trenches and take up fire positions. Elsewhere the *USS Cormack* had been shelling, blind, without success, the artillery battery a few thousand yards behind the line, which was causing havoc at the top of the E 1 draw. It gave up at about 0600hrs. At this time there were individual guns from five American artillery battalions ashore, but their combined losses had been over twenty-six guns and a mass of equipment. As such these battalions were able to play very little part in the days fighting and counter-battery work was impossible. However, engineers, unruffled by the enemy fire, completed the clearing of three gaps partially opened at low water in the morning, made four new gaps and by evening thirteen gaps had been cleared and marked. 40% of the beach obstacles had now been removed. Whilst this was happening engineers of the 1st, 37th and 149th Battalions had cut a road up the E 1 draw towards St Laurent, which they finished just after 1300hrs and straightway vehicles began their move up, only to be stopped by fire coming from the village. The draw was jammed but by 1600hrs a side road had been hacked out towards the adjoining fields and this was used to good effect. At 1700hrs the remaining tanks of 741st Battalion were ordered up the draw and four of these tanks took part in an unsuccessful attack on St Laurent that evening.

Colleville - pre-war

THE END OF THE DAY

A glance at the usefulness of the other exits at the time would have revealed that the Vierville draw was partly open but blocked by fresh debris from enemy artillery fire. This was cleared by 121 Engineer Combat Battalion just before nightfall and the draw used by part of 743 Tank Battalion to reach a Lager area north of the village by dark. The D 3 draw was still blocked. At E 3 enemy artillery caused innumerable delays on the engineer working parties but, with nightfall this fire slackened and tanks were able to be pushed up the draw at midnight. As dusk fell that evening the dark grey clouds seemed to lower themselves and at the beginning of a wet night it appeared that only a start had been made in clearing and organising the beach. The main transit area north of St Laurent was still jammed by nightfall as was the sand near the E 1 exit. A large number of miss-landed troops from all Arms and Services who had been landed during the day in the wrong places were still trying to find their parent units. They dug-in where they could and hoped for a better day. Up on the bluff top an area about two thousand yards deep had been taken at Collevile and very much less at St Laurent and Viervillle. The whole area was still within effective artillery range from well sited enemy gun positions. It seemed a somewhat gloomy picture particularly when it was known that medical supplies were, amazingly, virtually non existent and casualty clearing stations had been unable to set up. The logistic plans had called for 2400 tons of supplies to be landed that morning. Little more than 100 tons had been unloaded on shore. The ammunition supply was therefore critical and would have been much worse had not some 90 of the 100 pre-loaded DUKWs arrived on the beach successfully. The planned basis for logistic organisation was plainly not in place, a fact that presaged further delay and disruption during the coming days. Material losses had been considerable including over 50 tanks. There are no records available for vehicle losses except those for the 4042 Quartermaster Truck Company which lost 22 out of its 35 trucks that day. The Navy lost about 50 landing craft and ten larger vessels.

Some of the first casualties

The reckoning

The official casualty estimate on D + 1 was 3,000 killed and wounded most of whom were lost in the first few hours. This surely must be wrong when notice is taken not only of the strength of the enemy but also of German accounts of the battle. The beaten zones of over one hundred machine guns which lined the top of the bluffs would almost certainly have accounted for many more than 500 dead if the ratio of 15% is taken as reasonable. This 15% is a depressingly accurate estimate on the relationship between killed and wounded in every conflict since the Franco Prussian War. German soldiers who lined the bluffs that dreadful day and who were behind the machine guns reckon that the dead must have numbered well over 2,500 but put the casualties to 6,000 plus.

Perhaps it was politically impossible for Gerow to confess to such a blood-bath. Perhaps there were other reasons to conceal the true figure, one of which may have been the effect on public opinion back in the USA?

We can leave this desolate scene with a first hand description by a platoon commander. *"My landing craft came in as dusk was falling. I leapt off quickly into knee-deep water and started to wade towards the shore near the Casino Hotel. I looked down, I looked down again and realised that I was moving through a thick, pinkish soup of tattered human remains and bits of anatomy. The memory haunts me to this day and I do not wish to come back, ever. The place was a hell-hole"*

Dead awaiting burial

D + 1. A French welcome

Epilogue

It is permissible, sometimes, to have hindsight. Perhaps the decision to land the forward divisions at half light, due to the need for tactical surprise, was a bad one? It ignored years of experience gained at very high cost in the Mediterranean and Pacific but achieved a consensus of Allied opinion on the basis of erroneous compromise. This was wrong and Gerow and Huebner should have been allowed very much more influence on a decision with which they thoroughly disagreed. Bradley's unfortunate statement *"You men should consider yourselves lucky. You are going to have ringside seats for the greatest show on earth ..."* and the general opinion *"that the assault would not be too difficult... against an unprepared enemy of poor quality"* deepened the shock that veterans and inexperienced soldiers felt in the situation on OMAHA Beach. The stark difference between what they had been led to expect and what they saw may well have accounted for the paralysis on many parts of the beach that morning. The paralysis was caused by the mind's failure to comprehend the situation the eyes beheld or, in more modern terms, cognitive and sensory overload or acute stress-induced psychosis. The ever-present threat of a violent death, the noise and the sight of mangled bodies of both friend and enemy became too much for the uninitiated mind to comprehend. Mostly, this paralysis, this cognitive overload was a temporary infliction and after a short time the majority of men accepted the situation and, perhaps, were able to spur each other into action.

For a few, the paralysis was deepened by the soldiers' inability to either advance or retreat and many undoubtedly suffered from psychological dislocation which became permanent psychological scarring. Perhaps this afflicted the inexperienced more than the veteran. Why, it may be asked, was an inexperienced division, the 29th, put into this hell-hole when, from the very conception of the outline plan, it was agreed by all the joint-planners on the COSSAC staff that the initial invasion should be conducted only by battle-hardened troops? Thus, why was the experienced 9th Infantry Division, back in England. not used ? The 9th, *The Old Reliables* as they were called, had acquired battlefield skill in both North Africa and Sicily. Furthermore the 9th had joined a Marine division on amphibious training in the Pacific in 1941. Should it not have been sent to OMAHA in place of the 29th?

A captured chicken - an interlude of peace

Finally two more factors in a situation whose influence cannot truthfully be gauged: *The greatest amount of air power ever assembled allied with the enormous initial fire power provided by the navy* were found to be inadequate: the first by excuse-wrapped incompetence and the second through a paucity of large ships firing too few shells over too short a time from a position too many miles from an unobserved target. This should not have happened – the clear lessons gained at such cost in the Pacific and in the Mediterranean had been published for all to see but little attention had been paid to them.

Lastly, the commander, Leonard Gerow, had never fought a Corps or a Division in battle. Unwanted by his junior, Bradley and described by Patton *as one of the most mediocre corps commanders in Europe*, he was perhaps too old at 54. But he understood better than his superiors the near impossibility of breaching the beach obstacles that would later cause such havoc and delay. He wanted the assault to start one hour before low tide as opposed to two and a half hours before high tide so that he could have time to clear these obstructions when they were dry. In this he was supported by Admiral Hall – but their request to Bradley never received serious consideration. Unwisely, Gerow did not force the point although he had every opportunity to do so.

Perhaps, unfairly, on this evidence Gerow has become the convenient scapegoat that his superiors and almost everybody else sought. But it must be borne in mind that the first few hours of the assault bogged-down, and the casualties mounted, because of the inability of the amazingly brave engineers and under-water demolition teams to clear most of the obstacles in the insufficient time available. It is, then, Bradley who should shoulder the greater part of the blame for the near-defeat and unacceptable casualties on OMAHA Beach that June morning. The bravery and tenacity of those courageous young men on OMAHA Beach may have redeemed Gerow, and Bradley – but that was a bill that should not have been theirs. That price was much too high.

And, finally, lunch!

ACKNOWLEDGEMENTS

A large part of my life has been spent as a soldier and a much smaller part living in France, not far from Omaha Beach. As a product of Stowe, Exeter University, Balliol College Oxford and the Staff College. I seem to have been Tolstoy's perpetual student – hence the book has been written as the product of two careers.

I would like to pay tribute to two particularly good friends. The first, Dr Carlton Joyce, has shared unstintingly his great knowledge of the United States Army and its battles in Normandy. The second, Norman Machin, has put me in his debt by reading and commenting on the manuscript. To Nathalie Worthington, Franck Marie, Isabelle Catherine and Christophe Prime I extend my thanks for bearing with me and for offering friendly advice when needed. Space prevents me from mentioning all the help I have received from Omaha veterans. They call themselves " just ordinary men " but ordinary men they are not – they are gentle, kindly people who have been very willing to help me, as have research institutes and libraries, the US D-Day Museum, the RUSI and the keepers of German archives. Since there is no space for a bibliography I do hope they will accept this inadequate thank you. Of course, the mistakes are all mine.

O.B.W.

GLOSSARY

AVRE
Armoured Fighting Vehicle Royal Engineers Battalion
Battalion - basic Infantry unit in all armies in Normandy approx 650-850 men

Corps
A group of divisions, usually three, normally under command of a Lt General

DF
Defensive fire

Division
A formation, normally commanded by a Major General, of three Regiments
amounting to between 12500 to 18000 men

DUKW
Duplex drive amphibious truck

HE
High explosive

LCA
Landing craft Assault

LCI
Landing craft Infantry

LCT
Landing craft Tank

LCPV
Landing craft Vehicle and Personnel

LST
Landing ship Tank

ML
Motor launch

Regiment US
Equivalent to a British Brigade of three battalions and supporting arms

Photographic Credits

legal deposit: march 2004
© 2003-2004 Éditions du Mémorial de Caen
Designed by:
ATYPIK > 02 31 41 61 81
Fontaine - 14170 EPANEY
Printed in France by:
GRAPH 2000 > Argentan